D0582131

the *Ann Summers*
little book of
sex

the *Ann* Summers
little book of
sex

EBURY PRESS
LONDON

First published in 2001

18 19 20

First published by Ebury Press
Random House, 20 Vauxhall Bridge Road, London SW1V 2SA

Random House Australia (Pty) Limited
20 Alfred Street, Milsons Point, Sydney,
New South Wales 2061, Australia

Random House New Zealand Limited
18 Poland Road, Glenfield, Auckland 10, New Zealand

Random House South Africa (Pty) Limited
Endulini, 5a Jubilee Road, Parktown 2193, South Africa

The Random House Group Limited Reg. No. 954009

www.randomhouse.co.uk

A CIP catalogue record for this book is available from
the British Library.

ISBN : 9780091882372

Art direction and design by Blackjacks Ltd
Designed by Johnny Pau
Make-up by Bettina Graham
Photography by John Freeman

Printed and bound in Singapore

contents

foreword

*Welcome to The Ann Summers Little Book of Sex.
Inside you'll find plenty of tips and ideas to help
spice up your sex life and hopefully stimulate you
to experiment a little more!*

*Relationships can grow stale over time, especially
if your sex life is repetitive. Trying out new sexual
techniques and accessories will add a magic
spark back into your sex life. There is something
for everyone here, whatever your taste or desire,*

from foreplay techniques through to ideas for fulfilling lifelong fantasies and dreams.

Remember, you only live once and you may not know what you're missing...

Jacqueline Gold

Chief Executive, Ann Summers

forepl

Foreplay means different things to different people. It can mean everything we do before intercourse or specific actions, like kissing, massage, oral, or manual stimulation. In fact everything we do after meeting a sexual partner could really be called foreplay: the way we dress, walk, smile, use make up or after-shave. An enormous amount of human behaviour is dedicated, consciously and unconsciously, to foreplay as a prelude to sexual intercourse. For many thousands of years, humans have been turning foreplay into an art form and we continue to invent new ways of interacting with our partners so that sex, when it actually takes place, will be even more exciting and special. Let your imagination run riot and see what happens!

ay

flirting

Flirting is an intrinsic part of nature, and not only human nature; many birds and animals alter their behaviour in order to attract a mate, even when that mate is one they've had for many years. Women and men of all ages flirt most of the time, not always consciously, but many couples stop flirting once they're established in a relationship, and then wonder why the original fun and spontaneity have gone. Continuing to be flirtatious with your partner, and letting them know you find them attractive, is an important part of maintaining an enjoyable sex life - it's also great fun!

Foreplay as a prelude to sex can start anytime and anywhere you want it to, so you don't have to wait until you get home from an evening out to start having fun together. Until quite recently 'making love' simply meant paying loving attention to someone, and you can let your partner know how much you want her or him long before you start to touch or undress. Eyes can say almost everything, so let your lover know what's on your mind, by looking at him across a table, or across that crowded room. Over dinner or a drink, in a cinema, or just walking along

the road, start to show how
you're feeling. You can brush
fingers, hold hands, put your

arm around them and
whisper what you'd like to do
when you get them home.

getting it
together

Delaying gratification is a
sure way to arouse a lover.
It can of course be great fun
to rush into the house and
instantly make love, but then
it's over very quickly and the
night is still young. Agree to
take it slowly. Turn down the
lights, turn up the heating
if it's chilly outside, light
candles or incense, run a
scented bath, get out the
massage oil, and the sex

toys, bring the quilts and cushions from the bedroom and put them in a place with plenty of space that you've maybe not explored before. You want to use all your senses to please your lover and be pleased in return, so find a special location that isn't the bedroom.

Undressing can either enhance or totally ruin a sexual mood; it should appeal to the eye and be a turn on for both partners. Again, take your time, run your hands all over your body before undoing anything. Lift your shirt or skirt slowly and deliciously, don't struggle with it, grunting! Undo any buttons or zips provocatively and slide the fabric down over your skin. If you've planned in advance, you'll be wearing silk or sheer underwear that looks great and feels wonderful to the touch. Women, slide your bra strap down slowly over your shoulders; men, turn away as you remove your underpants and let your partner glimpse your buttocks. You can change the scene by undressing each other simltaneously or one at a time. One person being clothed and the other naked can also be an unusual and arousing situation.

Wash each other in the bath or shower without deep kissing or intimate touching and feel the excitement growing between you. Sensuous touching that avoids the main erogenous zones of lips, nipples and genitals is extremely arousing, and will leave your lover eager for more.

k

ssing

This is one of the most intimate things that it's possible to do with another person. For many people it's a much more intimate act than intercourse or oral sex. The mouth and lips are a major erogenous zone with a direct nerve link to the nipples and genitals. This link is stronger in some people than others, and it's not unknown for men and women to reach orgasm simply from kissing.

Kissing is usually mouth-to-mouth, but you can use your lips, tongue and teeth to explore every part of your lover's body. Start with the lips and brush them together gently. All parts of the mouth are highly sensitive, so use your tongue for exploration in a soft, relaxed way, then be harder in the technique and more assertive. Move to your partner's eyes, ears and neck. Men and women respond to nipple stimulation. Some women are able to have orgasms when their nipples are stimulated, while most men are unaware of just how sensitive and responsive their own nipples are to being sucked and caressed. Use your mouth to arouse all parts of your lover's body from the toes to the top of his or her head.

massage

Massage isn't just for fun, it really can help you feel more relaxed, less tense after a day at work, and more ready to enjoy sex with your partner. It's also a lot easier to do than most people realize, and giving a massage can be just as exciting and stimulating as receiving one. Using a massage oil makes it easier and more comfortable, and it also benefits the skin,

making it desirably smooth and soft. You can find good oils in most shops or you can make your own from culinary varieties such as olive or groundnut, adding essential oils to stimulate your sense of smell. Use sensuous scents that complement your mood - if you want relaxing or fresh use lavender or grapefruit, for heady and languorous use oils like sandalwood or cinnamon.

Make sure you're in a warm, comfortable environment where you won't be disturbed, and that your partner is lying on a firm mattress or futon that is covered with a towel. Rub

some oil into your warm hands and then run them over your partner's body, as they relax on their front, beginning with light, feathery touches. Slowly build up your movements, and don't be afraid to use all parts of your hands, including the edges, wrists and knuckles. Feel for the parts of your lover's body that seem the most tense, perhaps the shoulders or neck, and using circular thumb motions ease the stiffness out of the muscles. Make sure you soothe all those areas that you wouldn't usually pay much attention to during lovemaking: the back, the ankles, the feet and the shoulders. The face and head in particular are highly responsive.

You can take it in turn to give each other a massage, or one

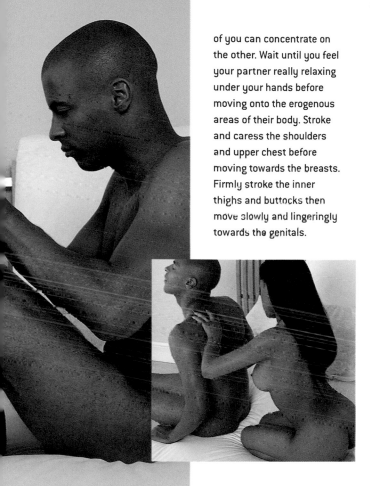

of you can concentrate on the other. Wait until you feel your partner really relaxing under your hands before moving onto the erogenous areas of their body. Stroke and caress the shoulders and upper chest before moving towards the breasts. Firmly stroke the inner thighs and buttocks then move slowly and lingeringly towards the genitals.

pleas

uring
ourself

Many people of all ages grew up with the idea that giving themselves sexual pleasure was 'sinful'. These attitudes are changing very rapidly, and these days, giving yourself an orgasm is considered an entirely 'normal' activity. In fact, giving yourself pleasure has all kinds of psychological and physical benefits, including increased self-confidence, better circulation and sharper mental activity. Self-pleasure can mean a quick orgasm; it can also mean a lengthy session of self-loving. Start by making yourself comfortable, maybe have a bath, light some candles. Do all the things for yourself that you would do for someone else. Begin by touching yourself gently, exploring the familiar erogenous zones as though for the first time. Avoid your clitoris or penis for as long as you can, instead massage your testes or labia, your perineum or anal area. Run your hands over your abdomen and nipples, and remember that your whole body is a sexual organ, not just your genitals. If you use toys (see page 76 onwards), make sure they are close to hand with lots of lubricant. Go slowly, this is something to be enjoyed - a pleasure just for you.

pleasuring your partner

Learning the art of self-pleasure is essential for full sexual enjoyment with a partner. Improving your pleasure skills with yourself naturally improves your skills with a lover; it also ensures that you are more independent and less demanding of satisfaction which in turn creates less pressure on both of you. You may not always want to have penetrative sex with your partner and knowing how to satisfy them manually and orally is an essential skill for a complete sexual life. Oral sex in particular can be highly erotic.

Women can begin by stroking their partner's thighs, abdomen and chest. Play with his nipples until they begin to harden, draw your fingernails lightly down towards his groin then run them up between his legs avoiding his penis. Brush your

fingers over his perineum and anus. Gently massage his scrotum, watching his reactions to see if what you are doing is pleasurable. Some men have very sensitive testes, others enjoy quite hard stimulation, but always make sure you know what your partner enjoys before getting rough. Tickle him lightly along his flanks, occasionally touching his penis as if by accident. If his own hand moves towards his penis, slap it away - you're in charge! When he's starting to wriggle with frustration, run your hands lightly up the length of his shaft and begin to move your hand rhythmically, squeezing slightly as you do so. Try using a water-based lubricant, your movements will be much smoother and more sensuous; some are even flavoured for oral pleasure too.

Oral sex is also know as a 'blowjob', but if you want to

please your partner, suck, don't blow! The head and frenulum (foreskin attachment) of the penis is particularly sensitive and this is a good place to begin using your tongue and lips with gentle lapping and sucking movements, while continuing to caress his penis and scrotum. Vary what you do at first, gently take his testes in your mouth and caress them with your tongue if this is something your partner enjoys. Run your tongue along his perineum and inner thighs if he seems to be getting too excited too fast. If you're able to take all his penis into your mouth and continue sucking and licking, then do this. Many men find the feel of their partner's lips around the base of their penis very erotic, but don't force

it until you choke or gag as that's no fun for either of you. Create some variety with your lips, tongue and even teeth, and as your partner gets more excited, start a rhythmical motion with your head.

Some women enjoy their partner ejaculating in their mouth, others do not. If you don't want your partner to come in your mouth make this clear before you start, or simply withdraw and use your hand, or surprise him with the Shakti position (see page 59).

Your man can start pleasuring you by stroking and caressing your whole body, sucking your nipples and running his tongue over and under your breasts, while placing his hands over your abdomen. Let him stroke and lick your inner thighs from just above the knee, moving upwards slowly and teasingly. Men, take your time, don't rush

towards her vulva - the whole genital area is highly sensitive, not only the clitoris and vagina. Massage the pubic bone with the palm of your hand, then lightly run your fingers over the outer labia and towards the perineum and anus. With

one hand open the outer labia and begin caressing the inner lips; use only gentle movements at first. As your partner begins to become more lubricated, move towards the opening of the vagina and explore it, teasing her by starting to penetrate her with a finger or two then withdrawing. While stimulating her vagina with one hand, begin light circular

motions around her clitoris with your other hand or tongue. Some women enjoy gentle, feathery motions on their clitoris, others prefer harder, pressured movements. Watch her reactions and if you're unsure, ask what feels good. Use your lips and tongue to suck and lick the entire vulva area, probe her vagina with the tip of your tongue; avoid using your teeth unless you know she likes that.

As she becomes more excited, use rhythmical lapping or sucking motions with your tongue or lips on her clitoris which will become swollen and engorged. Some women like to concentrate on clitoral sensation alone,

others find it easier to achieve orgasm if they are penetrated vaginally or anally as well, so use your fingers in gentle pumping motion, or a harder thrust, whichever she prefers. You can also use a dildo or vibrator to stimulate her vagina while you caress her clitoris, or vice versa. If you both want intercourse, wait until immediately before

she reaches orgasm then move smoothly and quickly into the Missionary position (see page 52) for simultaneous ecstasy!

game

Just because we grow up doesn't mean we have to stop playing. As adults our potential for games is even greater than it was when we were children because we have a wider range of experience and imagination to draw on. What children have that we as adults probably lack, is a sense of wonder and openness to the possibilities of game playing. To enjoy ourselves to the full we need to revive that potential. Try out some things that you may not have considered before, reverse expectations when you make love with your partner and surprise him or her in unexpected places.

dress for excess!

Sex doesn't always have to be about getting naked. One of the most fun games adults can play is 'dressing up' for sex. It can make us feel attractive, different; it can help to turn our partner on and it can remind us of the excitement of fancy-dress parties when we were kids! 'Dressing up' can be as simple as wearing an overcoat with nothing underneath, or stockings and suspenders without knickers. At the other extreme it can be about total disguise, using masks, body-paint, or hired

costumes and wigs. Clothes can help your favourite fantasies come to life and make any game seem much more exciting and real! Whether you're a man or a woman, seduction is an important part of adult games and feeling that you look the part, even if you're only wearing a brief towel round your waist, or high-heeled shoes, can really add to your enjoyment and confidence.

Rubber and leather are perennial favourites for sex-costumes, as are French-maid's outfits, thigh-high boots and stiletto-heeled shoes. Everyone has different fantasies and you and your partner could have a lot of fun together just talking about what you enjoy and planning a fantasy evening or weekend away. Remember, you can be anyone you want in fantasy-land: slave girl or boy, or rulers of the universe!

In a variation on dressing up, wear your oldest most worn-out clothes and then, as things hot up between you, simply rip or cut them off! How often have you wanted to 'get at' your partner but had to wait while he or she carefully removed their clothes? Pulling a shirt or dress off with your bare hands can be a really liberating, fun thing to do, especially if you're someone who normally folds everything up really neatly!

bondag

One of the most common sexual fantasies for both men and women is being controlled or restrained. Luckily this is one of the simplest and most fun to experiment with. Bondage, when you tie up your partner, restricting movement, can be very easily achieved using anything from a stocking or a tie, to handcuffs or rope. For women and men who can feel shy about their bodies or sex in general, having control taken away from them can often be very liberating. If other things are added, such as blindfolding, then the experience of being touched and explored can be very intense. Many men find enforced passivity relaxing as well as very exciting, and for both partners it can be a fun way to experience personal fantasies. You could experiment with a simple scarf tied around the wrists. If you have bed posts try tying your partner's wrists and maybe ankles to each corner. You can have hours of not-so-innocent fun experimenting with equipment and locations!

35

sub
& d

mission
omination

Power and sex have been linked probably since humans evolved. The advent of AIDS in the 1980s has required sex to be safer, but with greater imagination. Today, games of domination and submission are an increasingly popular way for couples to enliven their love life by introducing role-playing which allows both partners to express individual or mutual fantasies.

Sub/dom, as it is also called, is a psychological fantasy in which one partner controls

the other, either physically and/or sexually. This control may be 'forced', through blindfolding, or restraining

the partner with handcuffs, rope or a stocking; it may be through threats of 'punishment' with a whip or belt. There are many possible forms of playing together; experiment until you find what suits you both best. Domination is often linked with sado-masochism, but it is quite a separate game and need not involve pain, or even the threat of it. Simply

teasing, withholding sexual contact, or preventing orgasm can be a means of control. Being forbidden to touch your partner or yourself while being driven crazy with lust can be very, very exciting. For some people, however, pain can be sexually stimulating; for others it's a complete turn-off. If you are interested in the sado-masochistic elements of sexual games, discuss this in depth with your partner and find out what works for you both.

Exploring your fantasies with your partner can be a very intimate experience and, for the submissive partner, handing over control of physical freedom and sexual pleasure to the other person can be exciting, slightly scary and very stimulating. For some couples this may be

a good way of improving communication about what really turns you both on, and what turns you right off. Whether you are submissive or dominant in your role-playing, you may feel conflicting emotions at first. Be aware of this and only play games together when you are both feeling completely relaxed with each other. You may feel more comfortable in one or another role, but try to vary things. Perhaps one day you can be a slave being inspected and purchased in ancient Rome, but the next day you are the owner. You might be a queen and her footman, or a sultan and a harem girl. You can even try swapping gender roles. One of the most fun aspects of sub/dom is its theatricality.

upstairs - downstairs

Not all games need elaborate costumes or a scenario. There are plenty of ordinary household items which, with a little imagination, can provide hours of grown-up fun.

Food is one of the sexiest things around for many people and there are ways of combining food and sex that will appeal to you both. You could try tiny snacks or a whole meal! Not all sexy food has to be sweet. If you prefer something savoury why not try carpaccio of raw beef, or delicate piles of sashimi, or sushi, placed on your

partner's body - try salmon on the stomach, tuna on the breasts. Pick off each morsel with fine chopsticks and then dip in soya sauce. Delicious! Perhaps the most famous of all sex-foods, and a reputed aphrodisiac, is oysters. Some oysters are rich and creamy and melt in the mouth when bitten. Their texture is similar to the human tongue, so try sharing an oyster as you kiss, then wash it down with champagne. For dessert, chocolate sauce, ice-cream and small pieces of soft fruit make a particularly delicious sundae on your lover's skin. Try crushing raspberries between your tongue and her nipples, then feed them to her. Blindfold your partner then gently run pieces of ice or fruit sorbet over his chest and stomach, following that with a warm tongue. Finally, try an after-dinner mint. They're a great genital stimulant and create a powerful tingle! Suck one until there's only a bit left then go down on your

partner and wait for the gasp. Blow alternating cold and hot breath onto your partner's minty penis or vulva to

change sensation. When this trick was advertised on a local radio station in the USA, the county sold out of extra strong mints in a morning! Only mints containing real peppermint or spearmint oil work, but you can also experiment with crème de menthe which has the same localized effect and a real kick too.

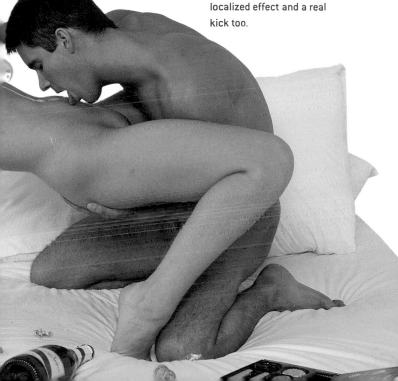

Mirrors can give an added, visual dimension to what you and your partner are doing, and they don't have to be on the ceiling! If you have a large mirror in the hallway, for example, move it temporarily into the bedroom where you can see it easily from the bed. If you have mirror tiles in the bathroom make love in the scented steam as you wait for your romantic bath together! Alternatively, use a large hand-mirror for close-ups of the action. Women, particularly, rarely see their genitals and it can be a turn on to view what's happening down there!

Ever thought of using a shaver as an erotic plaything? Shaving all or some of your partner's pubic hair can be great fun and you could make it a part of other games, such as Bondage (see page 34). Be sensuous and slow, massage shaving oil or cream into the skin; talk to your partner and say how it looks, what it will look like afterwards, how you're anticipating tasting and feeling the difference. Give them a hand-mirror to hold so that they can see exactly what you're doing. Bikini-line waxing is considered a normal part of grooming by many women, and as underwear for both sexes gets skimpier it's increasingly popular for both sexes to trim the hair between their legs. A growing number of men shave their scrotum and perineum as a matter of hygiene. (A useful male tip: trimming your pubic hair can make your penis appear larger!)

hot

46

positions

So how many sexual positions are there? It's a bit like asking how long is a penis? There's just no single answer. Some ancient Indian and Oriental texts suggest that there are as many as 1000 positions, others suggest 101. The reality is that there are a few basic positions with potentially endless variations. Below are some of the hottest positions around - a few are tried and tested, others are less well-known, some require a bit of athleticism! There are endless possibilities for coupling on chairs, stools, beds, tables, cars, or love swings. Find what suits you both best and experiment.

69

Just look at the shape of the number 69 and you'll get the idea! This is a position that many couples enjoy for itself, or as a prelude to penetration. Sixty-nine, or simultaneous, mutual oral sex, can be very intimate and tender or really wild with lots of action. It gives space for many kinds of fantasy and sensation, perhaps the wildest being that couples report getting so excited by the sensation of sucking and being sucked that they really feel the penis or clitoris in their mouth is where the sensation between their legs originates.

There are different ways of enjoying 69 and couples can experiment with what feels best for them. For example, you may want to place a pillow under the head and hips of the reclining partner. If the woman is on top she can fellate her partner deeply or quickly as she chooses, wrapping her arms around his hips and caressing his buttocks or anus; the man can wrap his arms around the woman's hips and draw her vulva down to his mouth, kneading her thighs or

48

stimulating her vagina or anus with his fingers. The kneeling partner can find the right angle and height to place their genitals above their partner's mouth without strain for either. With the man on top he can gently thrust into his partner's mouth, though not so deep or hard as to be uncomfortable. The woman can control her partner's movements by placing her hands on his hips and letting him know what feels good to her.

For a more relaxed version of 69, try the Golden Spoon, where both partners lie curled, head to tail, on their side with one leg bent flat and the other bent raised. Rest your head on your partner's inner thigh and nuzzle your way with lips and tongue. A way to enjoy hours of relaxing pleasure.

guys on

Probably the most universal sexual position, for many people the Missionary position with the man on top, the woman on her back is sex. The name supposedly appeared in the bad old days when Christian missionaries, confronted with 'native' sexual ingenuity, preached against having sex in ungodly positions, meaning anything other than face to face with the man on top. Happily, those days are gone. In this position the man can move easily without withdrawing and is free to change rhythm and speed; it can also be a very relaxing position for the woman as long as her partner takes his weight on his arms. A woman can still be active if she wants to, her hands can explore her own and her partner's body, stimulating nipples, clitoris and testicles. Many women find this a good position for orgasm if the man uses his pubic bone to stimulate the clitoris during penetration.

top

missionary

The Missionary is the basic position for many variations. The woman can caress her partner's thighs with her feet and legs, raising and thrusting with her hips, squeezing her thighs around her lover's hips and buttocks or wrapping her legs around his waist to allow deeper penetration and greater stimulation for her partner and herself. Some women like to raise their hips using pillows, which allows fuller access to the vagina and an exciting sense of exposure. Try it on deep fake fur rugs in front of a roaring log fire.

kneeling missionary

Want something face-to-face but raunchy and deeply penetrating at the same time? The Kneeling Missionary can be great for both of you because being on different levels, the man doesn't have to support his weight with his arms and has much more controlled drive, while the woman can wrap her legs round her partner's waist for really close action, or use the bed/chair/table/car bonnet to give her more thrust. Guys, try it kneeling on a cushion in front of a blow-up chair. Girls, try grabbing your ankles in each hand and really spreading those legs in the air!

54

emperor

The Emperor was named by Thai concubines many hundreds of years ago because in this position the man is both higher and in control. The man kneels back on his heels and the reclining woman pulls her knees towards her shoulders. Men, you can watch your own and your partner's genitals as they move together and it can give your partner a real sense of surrender and relaxation. Try lifting her buttocks and changing the angle of penetration, or lean forward with your hands on the back of her thighs for greater thrust. The woman can tickle and caress the man's nipples and lips with her toes, or lift her legs until her ankles rest on her partner's shoulders. A variation of this, the Lovers Knot, requires the woman to have a fairly supple pelvis. Here you start in the same position as the Emperor, but the woman places her feet firmly against the man's chest, and reaching between her thighs, locks her arms tightly around his waist. By pushing with her feet and pulling with her arms, the woman can lift and rotate her hips, controlling the degree of penetration and stimulation of her clitoris. The arms and legs are entwined like a 'knot' as you wrap and clasp each other.

catching the moon

An unusual variation of the man on top, Catching The Moon shown left, can develop from the Emperor or the Shakti position (see page 59).

Although the man is on top, it's the woman who has control of movement and speed. Holding his penis inside her, the woman lies back while her partner sits leaning forward, legs stretched out in front of him. The woman's legs are bent over the man's thighs and using her feet to push up off the surface, the woman can rub and thrust against her partner's groin while he kisses and caresses her nipples with his hands and tongue. In this position the man can move his hips only slightly but both partners can enjoy maximum stimulation.

splitting bamboo

Perhaps the 'hottest' position in terms of difficulty rating comes direct from the Kama Sutra and is called Splitting Bamboo. A more modern name might be Windscreen Wipers! To split the bamboo, the woman lies back with plump cushions under her pelvis while the man squats between her legs with a slight forward tilt. The woman then bends a knee and places one foot flat which the man holds by the ankle; the other foot is hooked over her partner's opposite shoulder or held upright in the air by him. Now comes the hard

part! At your own pace
assume the mirror
opposite position, i.e. the
man moves the woman's
legs from his shoulder, or
the upright position, to
the floor and back again
in a windscreen wiping
motion. Keep going as
long as you can.

on top

shakti

Now this is some guys' favourite position! The Shakti, named after the Hindu goddess, puts the woman in charge and lets the man lie back and enjoy being passive. The woman can choose the speed, depth and angle of penetration and discover what feels best. For many women this is the best position for orgasm as it's possible for them to stimulate their G-spot by angling their body so that the head of the penis is massaging low on the front (bladder) wall of their vagina. A woman can caress her partner's nipples and testicles. Try licking his neck or fingers and lean forward and tease his lips with your breasts. Men can relax totally, or thrust as much as the woman's weight will allow - stroke her breasts and caress her thighs. If the man is strong, or the woman small, he can lift his partner up and down on his penis using only his arms.

shears

There are a number of
variations on the Shakti, but
some require more flexibility.
In the Shears position, the
woman lies back from the
Shakti until her head is
between her partner's ankles.
This is a restricted position
for hip movement, but allows
easy clitoral stimulation by
the reclining man.

butterfly

The butterfly is another
variation. Keep one knee on
the bed and the opposite foot
stretched out like a sprinter

in the start position then draw your partner up towards you placing a hand under his lower back, rotating and plunging your hips. Then try it facing away from him - you'll find you're both stimulated in places you never knew existed. If you're an agile woman with flexible hips, try lying backwards onto the man's body from where he can caress your breasts and genitals.

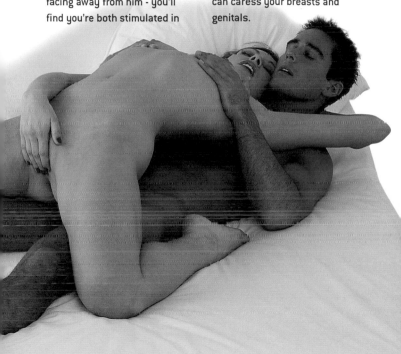

hot seat

A really 'hot' and complex facing-away position requiring flexibility and stamina in both partners is the Hot Seat. This starts with the man lying on his back then lifting his legs and opening them slightly. The woman lowers herself onto his penis, until she is sitting on the back of his thighs leaning against his feet. To stay steady, reach and clasp each other's wrists for balance. Alternatively, the woman can hold onto a strap or bar with one hand and, using her arms and feet, move up and down on her partner while stimulating her clitoris and the man's scrotum simultaneously with the other hand.

riding the wave

If you have endurance, experiment with Riding The Wave. The woman needs to place both feet on either side of the man's hips, then lower herself onto his penis, putting her hands on his chest for support or maybe linking hands with him mid-air for leverage, then go go go! Few men can resist the vigorous motion

and utter relaxation of being 'ridden' by their partner. Still being penetrated, the woman can lie back between her partner's open thighs and straighten her legs out, but be careful so that you don't strain his penis. From this position the man can sit up and a whole new position begins!

pet

positions

Have you ever watched animals mating in the zoo, the countryside, or on TV? Many animals engage in a whole variety of sexual activity, including sex for fun, for aggression, for tension relief and same-sex play too. Our nearest mammal relative, the bonobos ape shares almost 100 per cent of human genes. These creatures have sex - oral, manual and penetrative, heterosexual, homosexual and lesbian, in couples and groups - several times a day, for no obvious reason. They have it in every conceivable position... including swinging upside down in combinations

humans can only fantasize about! They also look deeply into each other's eyes as they do it. The happy bonobos are recorded as resolving all social conflicts through sex, and murder is unknown. Perhaps there are things we could learn from our nearest cousins. What have you got to lose? Be an animal!

hanging monkey

Primates sometimes mate face to face but usually face away, sitting on their haunches. Humans can try the Hanging Monkey position where the man kneels back on his ankles and the woman sits across him with her back to him. If the woman has a bar or strap to hold onto, as a monkey would hold a branch, she can move freely, raising and lowering her body and swivelling her hips. Primates often lick and rub each other as they mate; men can experiment with drawing their nails gently down their partner's stomach and back, or licking her neck and caressing her breasts.

doggie

The Doggie position is an old favourite with most mammals including humans and, yes, dogs! For human couples it involves the woman kneeling on all fours, while her partner 'mounts' her. Many women enjoy the idea of 'being taken from behind' and find rear entry especially stimulating as the penetration is

particularly deep. For a man this can be a powerful and dominating position which gives great freedom - so try caressing your partner's buttocks and anus and if you're agile, reach round and stimulate her clitoris.

sphinx

Big cats mate with the female lying down. In this position, known as the Sphinx, called the Piercing Tiger in ancient Hindu sex practice, a women can let fantasy take over. Unable to see your partner, or what

he's doing, your imagination is left completely free to roam. A male tiger mounts the female and grasps her by the back of the neck with his teeth so she can't get away and can't turn and bite him! Why not try it like the tigers, some playful biting and growling can be fun. Men can kneel on one or both knees to vary sensation. Women, lie on your stomach with your arms out in front of you, try it legs open on either side of his with back arched, or closed between his legs and squeeze!

folded serpent

Ever seen how snakes can bend into U-shapes? The Folded Serpent requires the woman to be able to bend right over and hold her partners ankles with her head between her knees. In this position the man is presented with an exciting and novel view of her vagina, anus and buttocks which he can stroke or playfully slap as you make love.

stand up for yourselves!

climbing vine

Straightforward standing positions can be complicated if the couple is very different in height, but one of you can always stand on a couple of big books or a small coffee table! Men, try lifting one of your partner's legs to allow greater access to her vagina and bend your knees if you need to adjust your height. If you're an athletic couple, or a big man and a small woman, you could try the Climbing Vine position which is a standing or crouching lift. If the man is strong enough he can lift his partner onto his penis while the woman grasps him around the waist with her legs. If this is difficult, try moving from a Kneeling Missionary into a crouching or standing lift; it can also help if the woman is supported by a wall, or holds onto an overhead bar or beam. If you're trying this outdoors, a tree branch would be perfect!

side to side

There are many sideways combinations but the basic positions involve a couple either facing each other, or facing in the same direction. Side-on sex can be good if you are pregnant, or just plain tired from trying all the other hot positions!

facing the world

It can be surprisingly difficult to manage penetration in a side-by-side, face-to-face position without some bending and curving of the partners' bodies. However, if the woman's legs are wrapped around her partner's waist and hips, things can

really start to move. You can kiss and hug each other and this is one of the few positions that gives a complete sense of mutual action. Women can try keeping one leg under their partner, one leg across his hip while arcing onto their back away from their partner, which allows him to thrust more strongly, using her raised hip for balance.

the cradle

Another variation of face-to-face is the Cradle, where the woman lies on her back, twists slightly and lowers both knees over her partner's hips as he lies on his side. He

then inserts his penis from behind while she keeps her legs tightly closed to hold him in and stimulate him further. This position allows face to face contact and can be particularly comfortable for pregnant women. In a variation of the Cradle, the man places his top leg between his partner's legs which gives deeper penetration and more stimulation to the vulva and clitoris from the movement of his thigh as he thrusts. The woman also has considerable freedom of movement in all these positions.

two spoons

The Two Spoons is probably the best known side-to-side position. Both partners lie on their sides with knees slightly bent, facing in the same direction, as the man fits into the contours of his partner's body. This is a very relaxing position for both partners as the man can thrust slowly and gently for long periods of time without tiring. He can kiss and lick his partner's neck, caress her breasts and clitoris, while she strokes his hips and flanks. Try angling away from each other so that the man can lightly scratch and massage the woman's back as he continues moving.

toys

Toys are not just for boys these days, in fact there's an almost limitless range of pleasure-tools out there for everyone to use. For example, dildos (or non vibrating vibrators), usually seen as women's toys, have a long and noble history dating back many years BC, and in many cultures are considered an art form. Today, they come in many shapes and sizes, from realistic penis types that 'ejaculate' to fanciful shapes such as dolphins or hands.

dildos

Dildos can enhance women's sexual pleasure in many ways, either during masturbation or with a partner. If you are enjoying sex alone, using a dildo for penetration can really enhance orgasm as you can control the speed and depth of penetration and still have one hand free for stimulating the clitoris or nipples. Dildos can be bought with suction cups and stuck pretty much anywhere for hands-free fun. A man can use a dildo to pleasure his partner, or because he's already ejaculated and isn't erect, or because he has difficulty getting an erection. Many men find seeing their partner penetrated in different ways very exciting. A growing number of men are discovering the male G-spot, the prostate, and the pleasures of anal penetration which can produce pretty ecstatic 'whole-body' orgasms. For women, penetrating

78

their partner can be a very liberating experience which promotes intimacy. Many women enjoy being penetrated anally and find it both excitingly different and relaxing. If you are both really into these practices and enjoy toys, there are many different kinds of strap-on and double-ended varieties of dildos to choose from. It can be very stimulating for both partners to experiment with mutual penetration, provided it's done gently and with lots of lubrication!

vibrator

You can find vibrators in many more shapes and sizes than dildos. They come in lots of different materials from metallic finishes and plastic to silicon and rubber-jelly. Some simulate the feel of real skin, others have a flexible moving foreskin. There are 'vibes' that glow in the dark, lipstick-shaped ones for clitoral stimulation, plenty of smaller models that fit perfectly in a handbag and lots in funky, bright colours that make them feel like a perfectly acceptable part of a modern woman's lifestyle.

Vibrators can also be used directly on the clitoris - there are hand-held types designed for use directly on the clitoris or penis or even for all-over body massage. There are even designs curved to hit the female G-spot.

of vibrator aims at three-way stimulation - a rotating shaft probes for the G-spot, rotating pearls stimulate the sensitive area around the entrance to the vagina, and a 'rabbit ears'-shaped attachment to the main vibrator shaft gives fantastic clitoral stimulation.

Nowadays most vibrators are battery-operated devices which allow greater freedom of movement. Hard plastic vibrators give the best vibrations but are noisier; denser materials tend to lose the good vibe you are after, but are quieter and therefore more discreet.

Many vibrators are also designed with variable speed settings so you can vary the intensity of stimulation. Some of the more sophisticated varieties aim to stimulate the whole genital area, with extensions for simultaneous clitoral, anal and vaginal stimulation. The 'rabbit' type

Many women who've never experienced an orgasm find it suddenly just happens when they use a vibrator - the stimulation is direct and can be very intense. A dildo can also be particularly useful as an introduction to anal sex for men and women. A low vibration rising to a more intense level can gently relax and loosen the anal muscles. If you're keen to try anal penetration, but are anxious about feeling discomfort, why not try it out with a small vibrator and lots of lubricant first. Try it on your own if you feel shy. Lots of cushions, a bottle of wine, good music - just you and the vibrator, alone, together!

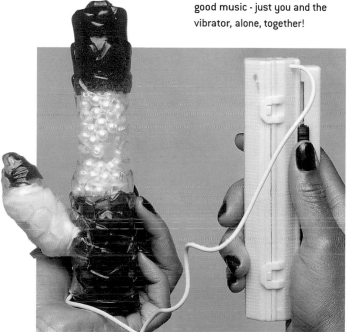

other toys

Everyone has heard of vibrators and dildos but there's a whole world of lesser known but equally fun toys out there just waiting to be discovered.

Ticklers, or sleeves, for example, are rubber sheaths with studs which can be worn over the penis during intercourse or over the finger for female masturbation. Clamps, or clips, can be used by women and men to intensify pressure and sensation in the nipples. If you're a woman who is into extra genital sensation, clamps can also be applied to the labia and clitoris. There are different types of custom-made clamps, from gentle rubber-tipped ones to crocodile teeth - only for the very serious! Try a pink plastic clothes peg and see how it feels...

Usually known as 'cock rings', penis rings fit around the base of the penis and prevent blood from draining too quickly, giving much harder erections. They can't slow down ejaculation, and they won't give you an erection if you don't already have one, but they'll certainly help you keep what you've got. For some men the feeling of size and 'fullness' adds sensitivity and enhances pleasure; rings can also reduce anxiety about losing the erection. Rings are usually made from rubber, leather or steel. Steel rings look great but can be very difficult to remove in a hurry and it's not a good idea to keep the penis engorged for more than 30 minutes at a time. Leather and rubber ones often have snap fastenings... or you could try a discarded stocking or bra strap! But never knot it so it can't be undone in a hurry.

'Jiggle balls' are a less well known type of toy. Inserted into the vagina, they give great sexy sensations as the balls, weighted with ball bearings, move about independently. Jiggle balls are also good for toning the pelvic floor muscles, which in turn can greatly enhance a woman's orgasm.

household

Ancient texts like the Kama Sutra advised lovers to break away from habits and routines and try new positions and locations to enhance sexual pleasure and physical and psychological health. Bed is great, but it's far from being the only place where sex can be enjoyed. Furniture is a wonderful and underrated sex toy. Remember those hanging basket seats with a strategically placed hole in the bottom?

Many couples use ordinary household or garden furniture as sex aids without even thinking about it. If you are serious about sex around the house and want something a bit different from the sofa or kitchen table, how about a love swing? Swings, or slings as they are also called, can be suspended from the ceiling, a tree, a beam... anywhere that will take a person's full body weight. Hindu illustrations of old sex guides show couples entwined on large swinging platforms. Today, swings come in all kinds of materials from leather to plastic, and allow one partner to be suspended in mid-air. A really good swing creates a weightless feeling that gives a couple the opportunity to experiment with positions that might otherwise be impossible. Swings can be used in many ways, for foreplay, penetration or just

fun

tickling. They can be hung at variable heights and used for everything from simply swinging through the air to full bondage. Most swings are portable, so with a little forethought and some very large hooks, you can hang out almost anywhere! Have you ever thought about those little household items that just might enhance sex for you both? There are endless possibilities. Feather dusters make great ticklers and feel wonderful against bare skin, as do those furry dusting 'gloves'. Don't forget your everyday leather gloves, either. An old scarf can make a great blindfold, a tie or tights a pretty good restraint.

BDSM toys

whips and paddles

Bondage, domination and sado-masochism may not be everyone's idea of a fun evening in (or out!) but if it's yours, there's a huge range of sex toys out there waiting to be explored and experimented with, whether you're a novice or an aficionado.

There are many different types of whips available, from fine fibreglass to heavy leather bull-whips and rubber cat-o-nine-tails. Whether you intend to use the implement or just threaten, sound is important and can add to tension and excitement. Paddles are flat, usually leather, and less 'severe' than a whip. Rubber whips are often more decorative than practical, but can be bought with attached rubber dildos for double fun!

restraints

Almost anything can be used as a restraint, from silk scarves or a pair of tights, to leather and steel manacles. Handcuffs are easily found and can be great fun for keeping your partner where you want them while you have your wicked way! Just don't lose the keys! There are leg-cuffs and 'spreader' cuffs, which have a wide metal bar between them designed to keep the feet apart. You can buy PVC body wrap on a roll. Cut strips to use as a restraint (or wind around the body to make sexy 'clothing').

Rope can be used for all kinds of bondage games, but remember it can chafe and burn. Also remember to never tie anything so tightly that it restricts circulation.

If you intend to do more than play with these items, remember that to mark or injure someone, even with their consent, is against the law in the UK.

health matters

safer sex

Everyone would like a problem-free sex life. One of the best ways to achieve this is to be aware of some basic health and hygiene precautions. Unwanted pregnancy, simple infections, Sexually Transmitted Disease (STDs) and HIV/AIDS can be prevented if you practise safer sex. Safer sex means not exchanging body fluids like semen or blood, which means that, to be safer, sex is non-penetrative, or done only while using a condom. Because condoms can break, no penetrative sex can be guaranteed as completely 'safe'. If you are in a long-term, monogamous relationship it is unlikely that you will need to practise safer sex, although hygiene practices still apply.

No-risk activities	Low-risk activities	High-risk activities
Caressing	Kissing	Anal or vaginal sex without a condom
Massage	Anal or vaginal sex with a condom	
Masturbation		Fellatio with ejaculation (especially if you have sore gums, ulcers etc)
Frottage (mutual body rubbing)	Fellatio	
	Cunnilingus	Drawing blood or sex during menstruation
	Inserting fingers into the vagina or anus	
	Using sex toys with a condom	

90

There are also basic rules of hygiene which should be followed by everyone regardless of risk of whether you need to practise safer sex with your partner or not. It is very easy to pass on minor infections such as thrush from one person to another so:

- Never put fingers/toys in a woman's anus and then into her vagina
- Never insert your fingers into your partner's anus/vagina and then into your own
- Never share dildos, vibrators or any toy without cleaning or changing condoms
- Don't engage in oral sex, either genitally or anally, without bathing first

Some people keep anti-bacterial wipes by the bed for just these kind of emergencies, but bear in mind that not all bugs will be killed. Remember that oral-anal contact (rimming) can transmit intestinal infections that no anti-bacterial wipe can eliminate.

condoms

These are available for both men and women, and if used properly, are very effective in preventing the exchange of semen or vaginal fluid. It's important to use them carefully to prevent splitting or tearing. Some men find condoms difficult to put on, or feel that they reduce their enjoyment. Condoms can, however, become part of foreplay and fun if both partners learn how to use them quickly and safely. Practise with each other before things get really hot and heavy, try unrolling a condom onto a banana or a dildo or squeezing and inserting a female condom in a sensual, erotic way.

The female condom is placed inside the vagina and held there by a flexible ring that fits around the cervix; it's held in place outside the body by a larger ring. It comes ready-lubricated inside, and is particularly effective in preventing infections of the external sex organs: the vulva and labia.

To insert, gently squeeze the smaller, insertable ring until it forms a narrow slit, then slide it as high as possible into the vagina while pushing down gently with the pubic muscles. The small ring expands inside the vagina and holds the condom in place, preventing it from sliding out during intercourse. Be careful when removing it not to spill any semen and to dispose of it safely.

Condoms for men have been around since at least the 17th century, and today are considerably more comfortable and effective than the sheep's intestines King Charles II reputedly used to prevent syphilis! There are many varieties of condom, available in all shapes, sizes and flavours; however many of these are not effective in preventing exchange of fluids. Only approved, kite-marked, condoms, within their sell-by date, should be used for safer sex.

After opening the packet carefully, squeeze the tip of the condom to prevent an air bubble which could burst the rubber during sex. Place the unrolled condom on the tip of the fully erect penis and begin to roll it down until it is right at the base of the penis. A condom that's too large or too small is ineffectual and can cause discomfort to both partners, so always make sure you get the right size for you (be honest!) and remember to hold the base of the penis and the base of the condom tightly when withdrawing to avoid any spillage.

Condoms are so widely used these days that they're having an effect on the environment, so rather than throwing them in the toilet where they'll remain in the system indefinitely, wrap them in toilet paper and put them in the bin for waste disposal.

index

Ann Summers, the fashion and passion retailer, specialises in selling lingerie, sex toys, fun novelties and accessories. The business was founded in the 1960s and quickly grew to become a brand name recognised around the world. Ann Summers has stores across the globe, hosts 4,000 Ann Summers parties per week and has one of the most successful websites on the internet.

The products featured in this book are available from Ann Summers. To order a catalogue or find out your nearest store, please call 020 8645 8399 or visit the website at www.annsummers.com.